MELTS

MELTS

FERN GREEN

MELTS

OVER 50 DELICIOUS TOASTED & GRILLED SANDWICH RECIPES

Photography by Jacqui Melville

hardie grant books

CONTENTS

INTRODUCTION

Welcome to the book of *Melts*: seriously tasty toasted (grilled) sandwiches; from classic cheese to pulled pork to breakfast hash ragu. Whether you are short on time or need a fantastic fill-me-up, here is a great selection of delicious melts to seduce your taste buds.

Factors such as the wrong cheese to bread ratio, and using poor-quality ingredients and unsuitable grilling methods can all produce sub-par toasties. Here are a few vital elements to help you build the best toastie or melt:

1. Your toastie has to be golden brown and crunchy. A soggy or burnt melt will have you shuffling it around the plate, and perhaps giving it to the dog. Salty butter spread over the outside of your sandwich combined with direct heat helps develop a magical golden crust. To add another dimension consider using a flavoured butter, with fresh herbs or garlic (see pages 20-22).

2. It's very important for your ingredients to have a savoury, salty lick as you want to be salivating and coming back for more after the first bite. When faced with a rich filling don't be shy to add a bit of acidity. Pickled vegetables are an important feature in a toastie; they cut through rich cheeses like there's no tomorrow. Check out the Pork Meatballs & Pickled Fennel with Walnut Pesto on page 56, Goat's Cheese & Pickled Beetroot on page 85, Spiced Stilton, Cheddar & Kimchi on page 89, and the Cream Cheese and Pickled Cucumber on page 90 for some good examples.

3. Bread. There is a definite need to hit the right mix of bread and filling. If the bread is too soft you may not get the right crust or chew. If the bread is too hard it might feel like biting down on a seriously fat crouton. As for freshness, one-day-old bread is the best. It will never be too soft and will crisp up like you want it to.

4. Don't feel that you need to go and buy a toasted sandwich maker. Most recipes here give you more than one option of how to make your melt. Some breads taste better under the grill, others browned in a toaster or pan-fried until crispy. Here are the possible cooking options that are given in each recipe:

🅢 TOASTED SANDWICH MAKER

These machines cut and seal your sandwich while toasting them before giving you the green light. These are great to use when your filling is slightly runny – baked beans don't usually behave themselves, but they do in one of these.

🅟 PANINI PRESS

These café-style toasters are brilliant for most melts. Even if you change up your bread and use a ciabatta roll or brioche bun they really look the part.

🅕 FRYING PAN (SKILLET)

No machine needed, just a heavy-based frying pan or griddle pan. Sometimes it helps to use a spatula to press down on the sandwich to get a crispy finish. Using a pan also allows you to keep an eye on your melt during the crisping up stage, as and when you want to.

🅦 WAFFLE IRON

A nifty utencil used to make waffles, which also works as a perfect sandwich toaster.

🅖 GRILL (BROILER)

The ideal way to make a toasted open-faced sandwich like the sticky sweet Cinnamon-Crusted Peach & Mascarpone recipe on page 128.

🅣 TOASTER

Simply toast your bread and top with whatever you fancy!

As well as the best bread and toasting options for each melt, the recipes also include approximate preparation and cooking times, so you can easily see which toasties can be made quickly and which take a bit more TLC.

A final note on ovens: where an oven is used in a recipe, the temperature given is for a fan-assisted oven. If you do not have a fan oven then increase the temperature by 20°C (70°F).

THE BREAD

Bread is the all-important foundation to a good toasted (grilled) sandwich. To help you pick the perfect slice, here is a selection of choices with a handy description of what works and why.

The White Bloomer

This is the favourite: a lovely white, spongy, doughy bread. Classically used for the simple cheese toastie, especially when it's a day old. Make sure not to slice it too thick as you'll have more bread than filling, but thick enough to envelop the cheese. The bloomer does not pack a punch in terms of flavour, but this is good as you want it to merely be a subtle vehicle to hold that lovely gooey cheese. Poppy and sesame seed covered bloomers enhance your melt, so don't avoid them. It doesn't half make a good golden crust too!

The Sourdough

The textural confidence in a sourdough is ideal for a heavy load-bearing toastie. It can support strong flavours, especially if it's made from rye flour, and creates a superb crunch. The occasional holes in the bread are a bonus when you have a cheese filling; the cheese melts through the holes and crisps up, giving your melt that yummy, crispy, deep cheesy flavour. On the other hand, very holey bread could also cause you a few issues.

The Ciabatta

Crisps up beautifully on the outside and stays light and fluffy on the inside. This bread is a great support for very melty, drippy cheeses as the ciabatta cups around the filling and prevents any potential cheese leaks! It's also good for non-cheese melts, as its dual texture keeps you coming back for more.

The Multigrain, Granary and Multiseed

Packed with fibre and full of flavour when toasted, these breads cushion creamy ingredients really well. Not recommended for carb fillings as the sandwich becomes too heavy. Lighter, creamier fillings, perhaps with herbs or pesto, are a good complement to these great breads.

The Waffle

Made in the traditional way with batter, or with potato or cauliflower. The waffle is an excellent hot, crispy alternative to regular bread. It takes a bit more effort but is definitely worth the time. Great for breakfast, lunch and dinner, so no excuses – give it a go!

The Brioche

A very soft bread with a sweet edge. Brioche takes less time to toast than other varieties of bread, so lighter fillings are necessary. A perfect pairing for sweet things, making it a great vessel for fruit like bananas, and delicious with sweet spreads like chocolate. It's best cooked in a frying pan (skillet) so you can keep an eye on it.

TOASTING

To griddle or not to griddle. To deep fry, shallow fry or use a toastie machine. What is the best method, you ask? This can be dependent on ingredients and bread choice; their size, shape, melt potential, whether soft or hard, and cooked slow or quick. All these factors should be taken into consideration. Most of the toasties you see in this book were made using a griddle or a heavy-based frying pan. If you want to use your toasted sandwich maker, many of the recipes can be adapted for this. Check the symbols next to each recipe (listed on page 9) for a guideline on which toasting method to use.

When crisping up your sandwich, there are a few tricks to add to the pan or the bread before you apply the heat.

Butter or Oil

Spread this on the outside of the bread; it helps to crisp up the toastie, giving it the appetising golden glow and crunch. Use a spatula to press down on the bread, encouraging the golden effect. This can be key in transforming your sandwich from good to excellent.

Extra Coatings

Try rubbing a garlic clove on the outside of the toastie to give it an added layer of flavour. Grating cheese onto the bottom of the frying pan (skillet) before adding your sandwich on top gives it a special cheese crisp . . . dreamy! Another top tip is mashed potato. Yes, you heard it right: spread a little mashed potato over the outside of your toastie, fry it again and you've got yourself an added crisp (chip) flavoured dimension.

THE CHEESETASTIC MELTING GUIDE

It is clear that great cheese makes a great cheese melt. Whether it's a powerful vintage Cheddar, a cave-aged Gruyère or a slice of nutty Gouda, they are all delicious in their own way, but some are better at melting than others.

There is a general rule that semi-soft cheeses, like Emmental and Gruyère, always melt how you want them to. However, here is a helpful guide to put you on the right track when you choose a cheese for your melt.

CHOOSING YOUR CHEESE

When shopping for cheese, you can't necessarily tell by its appearance or from the nutrition label how it melts. Don't worry - here are three categories to help you decide: stretchy, smooth and non-melting. The recipes in this book use cheese from all three camps; there is not just one good cheese to make a good toastie.

Stretchy

Cheeses of this type are popular on pizzas and used for stuffing into croquettes or pies. They pretty much stay put when heated, so you don't need to worry about it melting everywhere. Light and creamy in flavour, when pulled they produce a lovely stretch, some as long as your arm!

Burrata
Fresh Cheddar curds
Mozzarella
Scamorza

Smooth

This is the largest cheese camp and often the most popular type for making a melt. When cooked, they are viscous, rich, flowing and blend well. These cheeses rock when it comes to melting. Don't be shy about mixing them up to achieve ultimate status.

Cheddar	Gouda
Emmental	Blue cheese
Fontina	Red Leicester
Gruyère	Brie
Havarti	Camembert
Taleggio	Manchego

Non-melters

Grilled, fried and baked: this is where these cheeses excel. Though they may soften when heated, they won't lose their shape. There are a few reasons why a cheese might not melt: one being if it's high in salt and another is if it has a high acidity. Although these cheeses don't melt, this doesn't mean they won't make a decent addition to a toasted sandwich.

Feta	Parmesan
Halloumi	Ricotta
Hard pecorino	Soft goat's cheese
Paneer	

COOKING

Preparation

It's a good idea to take the cheese out of the fridge an hour or so before you are ready to make your sandwich to bring it to room temperature. Doing this reduces the amount of time the cheese will take to melt. The shorter the cooking time, the less likely the cheese will get too hot and split.

Grated

Grating increases the surface area of the cheese, also reducing the amount of time it will take to melt. Handy! This means you can synchronise making your melt. If, however, you are using a semi-soft cheese then thin slices will do.

Heat

Very high temperatures can tighten the proteins in a cheese, which squeezes out the moisture and fat, giving you a rubbery, globular, greasy mess! This can happen with pizzas baked in a very hot oven … not the worst thing in the world but you do end up with a floppy pizza. A more gentle heat is best.

BUTTERS & CRUSTS

Adding a coating to the bread of your toastie is an easy way to elevate it by providing extra flavour or texture. Check out these enticing homemade butters, and special potato and cheese toppings. They are included in several recipes in this book, but you can easily add them to every one if you wish.

Bloody Mary Butter

Soft butter mixed with Tabasco sauce, tomato purée (paste) and Worcestershire sauce gives your grilled sandwich an umami tomato edge. Make it on the spot with these essential store cupboard staples. Spread liberally inside the sandwich before cooking for the best effect.

Herb Butter

Finely chop hardy herbs, such as lemon thyme or rosemary – delicate herbs, like basil, will burn – and mix them in some soft butter. Coat the outside of your bread, then after sizzling each side, boom – you've got yourself a special herb-flavoured toastie!

Spiced Butter

Mix a little paprika, salt and pepper with softened butter and spread onto the outside of the bread - not only do you intensify the colour and crispness of the toastie but you bring an extra flavour dimension too.

For your sweet treats, try adding cinnamon or nutmeg to the butter instead. This especially works on breakfast-style toasties with added fruit. Brioche loves it and so does chocolate.

Citrus Butter

Lime or lemon zest grated into butter gives bread a tangy taste and enhances luscious, creamy fillings. Try this with goat's cheese toasties, cream cheese and sweet melts.

Garlic and Chilli Butter

If you're making a melt for dinner, you may require a more savoury note. Try adding some grated garlic or chilli flakes to softened butter to enhance the flavour. Add more or less according to your taste, but be careful not to add too much – they are powerful flavours when spread on just one piece of bread. I find that half a clove of garlic for two toasties or half a teaspoon of chilli flakes is plenty, unless you love it mouth-burningly hot!

Potato Crown

This special trick creates an even crispier crust to your toastie. Grab some leftover mashed potato, spread it on the outside of your already toasted sandwich, and fry each side again until the potato is firm and golden. Extra crisp, extra flavour and great if you are extra hungry.

Cheese Crown

For all those big cheese fans, a little bit of grated cheese coated on to your toastie brings that extra flavour. Make your toastie, then swipe a knob of butter into a frying pan (skillet). Grate a hard, high-fat cheese, like Parmesan, into the pan in the shape of your bread. When it starts to melt and the fat begins to separate out a little, place your sandwich on top.

Press down with a spatula until the cheese coating turns golden brown. Take out the toastie and repeat the process for the other side. Don't worry: it may not seem very crispy at first, but wait until the sandwich cools a little... Bingo – a crispy, cheesy crust has formed!

SIDES

Melts can be complete meals when served with a delicious, freshly made side. Additional flavours and textures can enhance your crunchy, cheesy experience. We're all familiar with the classic tomato soup as an accompaniment to the toasted sandwich; dipping a simple cheese toastie into a creamy, rich soup is heavenly. However, more complex toasties deserve something more tangy and crunchy, so here are few colourful examples to try.

1 medium carrot

½ fennel

2 radishes

1 small beetroot (beet)

¼ small celeriac

200 g (7 oz) red or white cabbage

½ red onion

handful of mixed fresh soft herbs, e.g. mint, dill, parsley and basil

125 g (4½ oz/½ cup) plain yoghurt

2 tbsp olive oil

1 tbsp Dijon mustard

juice of 1 lemon

sea salt and freshly ground black pepper

SEASONAL SLAW

Whatever the season, there is always a bountiful supply of veggies you can trim and slice to make a delicious slaw. Use this recipe as your base and swap in other fruit and vegetables, such as asparagus, apples, raisins, spring onions (scallions) and celery, to suit the seasons.

By hand or using a food processor, finely shred or julienne the carrot, fennel, radishes, beetroot (beet) and celeriac into a large mixing bowl. Slice the cabbage and red onion as thinly as you can and add them to the bowl. In another bowl, mix together the herbs, yoghurt, olive oil and mustard and season to taste. Stir through the lemon juice and pour over the prepared vegetables. Mix thoroughly and serve.

1 lettuce, e.g. Little Gem, romaine, oak leaf or iceberg, roughly chopped or torn

handful rocket (arugula)

¼ cucumber, diced or shaved with a peeler

small handful of parsley leaves

VINAIGRETTE

¼ garlic clove, grated

1½ tsp Dijon mustard

2½ tbsp white wine vinegar

6 tbsp extra-virgin olive oil

½ teaspoon white caster (superfine) sugar

sea salt and freshly ground black pepper

GREEN SALAD
with THE BEST VINAIGRETTE

PREP TIME:
5 minutes

This is a simple green salad – but with this lip smacking vinaigrette, it cuts through a buttery, rich toastie perfectly. Use your favourite leaves, add some peppery rocket (arugula) and season well.

Make the vinaigrette in a large bowl by whisking all the ingredients together until fully combined. When you are ready to serve, add the salad to the bowl and stir through.

4

1 tbsp cornflour (cornstarch)

1 tbsp vegetable oil

1 tsp caraway seeds

pinch of freshly ground
black pepper

500 g (1 lb 2 oz) carrots, cut into
long 1 cm– (½ in–) thick fries

1 tsp sea salt

CARROT CARAWAY FRIES

PREP TIME:
10 minutes

COOK TIME:
40 minutes

These are easy to make and a great addition to your toastie. No
need for knives and forks; simply pick up your toastie with one
hand and a carrot fry with the other – winner!

Heat the oven to 180°C (350°F / Gas 4) and line a baking tray
with baking parchment. Mix the cornflour (cornstarch), oil,
caraway seeds and black pepper in a large bowl. Toss the carrots
in the mixture until they are thoroughly coated. Spread them out
on the baking tray and bake for 40–45 minutes, turning them
halfway through cooking. Remove from the oven, sprinkle with
the salt and serve.

THE CLASSICS

This chapter covers all the classic toasted sandwiches that you may or may not have made in your lifetime. If you haven't, here is your chance to complete this achievement. If you have, why not remind yourself how good they are?

2 medium slices white bloomer

1 tbsp butter, at room temperature

25–50 g (1–2 oz) sliced ham

60 g (2¼ oz / ½ cup) grated vintage Cheddar, or 30 g (1 oz / ¼ cup) grated vintage Cheddar plus 30 g (1 oz / ¼ cup) grated Gruyère

HAM & CHEESE

PREP TIME:
5 minutes

COOK TIME:
6 minutes

TOASTING METHODS:
F S P

BEST BREAD:
white bloomer

The most loved toasted sandwich, eaten by millions at any time of the day. If you can get your hands on a really good quality cooked ham and use your favourite vintage Cheddar, then it is hard to go wrong here.

Spread one side of each slice of bread with the butter. Turn the bread over so it is butter-side down. Top one slice with the ham, then the cheese, then cover with the other slice so that the buttered sides of the bread are on the outside of the sandwich.

Heat up a frying pan (skillet) over a medium heat and place the sandwich in the pan. Fry for 3 minutes until golden brown. Flip the sandwich over and cook for a further 3 minutes or until crispy and golden on the outside and the cheese has melted inside. Alternatively, cook the sandwich in a toasted sandwich maker or panini press.

160 g (5 oz) tinned tuna in spring water, drained

1 spring onion (scallion), finely sliced

1 celery stalk, finely sliced

½ tsp Dijon mustard

2 tbsp mayonnaise

drizzle of olive oil

squeeze of lemon

sea salt and freshly ground black pepper

2 tbsp butter, at room temperature

4 medium slices multiseed or brown bread

60 g (2¼ oz / 1½ cup) grated mature Cheddar

TUNA MELT

PREP TIME:
5 minutes

COOK TIME:
6 minutes

TOASTING METHODS:
🅕 🅢 🅟

BEST BREAD:
multiseed or brown

Great for kids and quick and easy to make. This classic melt contains ingredients that you can probably find in your store cupboard or fridge right now.

Mix together the tuna, spring onion, celery, mustard, mayonnaise, oil and lemon juice in a bowl and season.

Butter one side of each slice of bread and turn them over so the butter-side is facing down.

Spread half of the tuna mixture onto one slice of the bread and the rest on another slice. Divide the grated cheese over the tuna mixture, then place the remaining slices of bread on top with the butter on the outside.

Heat up a frying pan (skillet) over a medium heat and lay each sandwich in the pan. Fry for about 3 minutes on each side or until golden and the cheese has melted. Alternatively, cook the sandwiches in a toasted sandwich maker or panini press.

½ small brown onion, finely sliced

1 tbsp Worcestershire sauce

1 tbsp butter, at room temperature

2 slices granary or multiseed bread

60 g (2¼ oz) mature Cheddar, thickly sliced

freshly ground black pepper

CHEESE & ONION

PREP TIME:
15 minutes

COOK TIME:
6 minutes

TOASTING METHODS:
F S P

BEST BREAD:
granary or multiseed

What's best: white or brown onion, red or spring onion (scallion)? Do you prefer your onion caramelised or perhaps you are partial to a good onion chutney? Having tested a multitude of onion arrangements, this version tops it. Simple brown onion, sliced in half moons with a little British marinade.

Put the sliced onion in a bowl and stir in the Worcestershire sauce. Cover and leave to marinate for 10 minutes.

Butter one side of each slice of bread and lay butter-side down.

Put the cheese on one slice, then spoon the onions on top. Grind some black pepper over, then press the other slice over the onions, butter facing outwards.

Heat a frying pan (skillet) to a medium heat, then lay your sandwich in the pan. Cook for 3 minutes on each side or until the cheese is gooey and the outside is crisp. Alternatively, cook the sandwich in a toasted sandwich maker or a panini press. It is especially tasty served with brown sauce!

4 slices salami

1 small ciabatta, halved lengthways

1 ripe tomato, sliced

60 g (2¼ oz) fresh mozzarella, sliced

MOZZARELLA, SALAMI & TOMATO

PREP TIME:
5 minutes

COOK TIME:
6 minutes

TOASTING METHODS:
P F

BEST BREAD:
ciabatta

The colours of the Italian flag . . . If ever you go driving on the *Autostrade* of Italy, this is a popular panino found at most petrol (gas) stations. It is also now a top favourite toastie in many other parts of the world. If meat is not your thing, swap it out for a good layer of basil leaves.

Lay the salami along the cut side of the bottom half of the ciabatta. Add the sliced tomato on top, then the mozzarella slices. Close the sandwich.

If you have a panini press, use it to cook the sandwich until it is toasted on the outside and the cheese has melted on the inside. Alternatively, heat a frying pan (skillet) to a medium heat, then add the ciabatta. Press down on the sandwich using a spatula and cook for 3 minutes on both sides or until crispy and the mozzarella has melted.

1 egg

2 slices smoked
streaky bacon

3 thin slices brown or white bread

2 tbsp mayonnaise

small handful of iceberg lettuce

4 thin slices cucumber

small handful cooked
chicken pieces

few slices red onion

½ tsp Dijon mustard

large slice mature Cheddar

4 thin slices ripe tomato

sea salt and freshly ground
black pepper

THE CLUB

PREP TIME:
5 minutes

COOK TIME:
10 minutes

TOASTING METHODS:
G T

BEST BREAD:
brown or white

This sandwich, whether a double or triple decker, holds its origins in the USA. Now every hotel around the world has their own classic version. Time to make your classic right here.

Cook the egg in a small saucepan of boiling water for 7 minutes. Remove from the saucepan and place it into a bowl of cold water to cool. When cool, peel off the shell and slice.

Meanwhile, cook the bacon either in a frying pan (skillet) or under the grill (broiler) until crispy. Lightly toast the bread on both sides under the grill or in a toaster. Set aside.

Spread half the mayonnaise on one slice of the toast. Top with the lettuce, cucumber, chicken and onion. Place another slice of toast over the onion and spread it with the mustard, followed by the cheese, bacon, tomato and egg. Spread the final slice of toast with the remaining mayonnaise, close the sandwich (mayonnaise side down). To hold it together, stick a toothpick through it.

2 tbsp butter

4 slices white farmhouse bread, crusts removed

1 tbsp plain (all-purpose) flour

100 ml (3½ fl oz) full-fat (whole) milk

80 g (2¾ oz/⅔ cup) grated Gruyère

¼ tsp grated nutmeg

1 tbsp Dijon mustard

2 slices good-quality ham

sea salt and freshly ground black pepper

CROQUE MONSIEUR

PREP TIME:
10 minutes

COOK TIME:
15 minutes

TOASTING METHOD:

BEST BREAD:
white farmhouse

The French take on a ham and cheese toastie. Croque comes from the French word *croquer*, meaning 'to be crunchy'. The ever so delicious Gruyère makes this a total classic. I think there is enough room in this chapter for two ham and cheese toasties, don't you?

Set the grill (broiler) to a medium-high heat and line a baking tray with baking parchment.

Melt the butter in a small saucepan, then turn off the heat. Brush one side of each slice of bread with about half of the butter and grill (broil) the bread butter side up until golden, then set aside.

Stir the flour into the saucepan with the remaining butter to make a paste. Cook over a medium heat for 1 minute, stirring continuously. Gradually whisk in the milk and continue whisking until smooth. Reduce the heat and simmer for 4–5 minutes or until the sauce has thickened. If you find it splits and the fat starts to separate, don't worry; sprinkle in a little more flour and whisk it through.

Take the saucepan off the heat and stir in 30 g (1 oz) of the Gruyère until it has incorporated into the sauce. Add the nutmeg and Dijon mustard, then season.

Put the ham and the rest of the Gruyère on the untoasted side of one of the slices of bread and pop it under the grill for about 4–5 minutes or until the cheese has melted.

Top with the other slice of bread, toasted side facing out, and pour over the cheese sauce. Grill for about 5 minutes or until the sauce is golden and bubbling.

1 small chicken breast

1 small ciabatta

1 tbsp mayonnaise

2 thin slices fresh mozzarella

3 cherry tomatoes, sliced

sea salt and freshly ground black pepper

1 tbsp olive oil

BASIL PESTO

30 g (1 oz) basil leaves

45 g (1¼ oz/scant ½ cup) walnut halves

1 garlic clove, peeled

½ tbsp grated Parmesan

2 tbsp olive oil

2 tbsp groundnut oil

sea salt and freshly ground black pepper

CHICKEN & PESTO

PREP TIME:
10 minutes

COOK TIME:
25–35 minutes

TOASTING METHODS:
F S P

BEST BREAD:
ciabatta

Basil pesto is loved by everyone. Allow yourself to slather as much as you like over this tasty sandwich. No one is stopping you!

Preheat the oven to 190°C (375°F/Gas 5).

Lay the chicken breast on a piece of kitchen foil and gather the edges of the foil together to create a sealed parcel. Bake the chicken in the oven for 20–30 minutes, depending on the size of the breast, or until it is fully cooked all the way through.

Meanwhile, make the pesto and start building the sandwich. Blitz all the ingredients for the pesto in a food processor for 30 seconds. If you like it really smooth, blitz a little longer. Then halve the ciabatta lengthways and spread one half with 1 tablespoon of the pesto and the other half with the mayonnaise. Place a slice of mozzarella on each half of the bread.

Slice and season the cooked chicken breast while it is still hot. Lay the chicken on one half of the ciabatta and drizzle 1 tablespoon of pesto over it. Top with the tomatoes, season, then close the sandwich and brush all over the outside with the olive oil.

Heat a griddle or frying pan (skillet) until hot. Place the sandwich in the pan and cook for 3 minutes on each side or until the cheese has melted and the sandwich is hot. Alternatively, cook in a toasted sandwich maker or panini press. Serve warm.

6 slices smoked streaky bacon

1 tbsp butter, at room temperature, plus extra for frying

2 slices multiseed bread

2 medium eggs

4 slices Swiss cheese, plus extra grated cheese, to serve

ketchup, to serve (optional)

EGG, BACON & CHEESE

PREP TIME:
5 minutes

COOK TIME:
15 minutes

TOASTING METHODS:
F S P

BEST BREAD:
multiseed

The ultimate breakfast melt! Hungry, hungover or simply in need of an egg and bacon fix – here is the solution. Scrambled egg is an alternative option here if you prefer, but it's hard to resist a drippy fried egg.

Cook the bacon either in a frying pan (skillet) or under the grill (broiler) until crispy. While the bacon is cooking, butter both sides of each slice of bread. Set everything aside when done.

Melt some butter in a frying pan and fry the eggs to your liking. To get a runny yolk and crispy edges, lots of butter helps! Transfer the eggs to a plate and keep the pan over a medium heat. If there is still a lot of butter in the pan you can swipe some away with a piece or two of paper towel - be careful not to burn yourself.

Place both slices of the bread, in the hot frying pan and fry each side for a few minutes until golden and crispy. Lay 2 slices of cheese on each, then an egg and finally top with the bacon. Fry for 2–3 minutes until the cheese has melted. Serve the melt with an extra sprinkling of cheese and some ketchup, if desired.

Alternatively, assemble the sandwich as described above, but add an extra slice of bread to close the sandwich. Cook in the frying pan, or carefully transfer it to a toasted sandwich maker or panini press, and cook until crisp on the outside and melted on the inside.

2 pork sausages

1 tbsp butter, at room temperature

2 slices sourdough (use slices without too many holes) or granary bread

1 tbsp wholegrain mustard

35 g (1¼ oz / 1¼ cups) grated mature Cheddar

ketchup, to serve (optional)

SAUSAGE, CHEESE & WHOLEGRAIN

PREP TIME:
5 minutes

COOK TIME:
20–35 minutes

TOASTING METHODS:
🍞 🥪

BEST BREAD:
sourdough or granary

This trio of flavours creates a great toastie, hitting all the savoury spots. When biting into this, close your eyes and it will send you to a place of happiness.

Cook the sausages using your preferred method, then set them aside. Meanwhile, butter the outside of each slice of bread.

Heat a frying pan (skillet) over a medium heat and spread the unbuttered side of one of the slices of the bread with the mustard. Place the bread butter-side down in the pan.

Cut the sausages in half lengthways and lay them on the mustard. Sprinkle the Cheddar over the sausages and press the other slice of bread on top, butter-side up.

Toast for 2–3 minutes, then flip the sandwich over. Cook for another 3 minutes or until the cheese has fully melted and your sourdough is lovely and crisp. Alternatively, assemble the sandwich as described above and toast it in a panini press. Serve with ketchup on the side, if desired.

1 tbsp butter, at room temperature

2 medium slices white bread

30 g (1 oz) baked beans

30 g (1 oz/¼ cup) grated mature Cheddar

sea salt and freshly ground black pepper

BEANS & CHEESE

PREP TIME:
5 minutes

COOK TIME:
5 minutes

TOASTING METHOD:
𝕊

BEST BREAD:
medium sliced white

This toastie is best made in a toasted sandwich maker like a Breville. Beans like to escape and create a bean mess all over your pan. Don't let this put you off, though, as this is up there as one of the best toasted sandwiches ever. Please note that the beans come out very hot from the toastie machine, so let the melt cool for at least a minute or two before biting into it.

Heat up the toasted sandwich maker.

Meanwhile, butter the bread on one side, then lay the slices butter-side down. Carefully spoon the baked beans onto one slice of the bread, sprinkle the cheese on top and season. Lay the other slice over the cheese with the butter side facing up and carefully transfer the sandwich into the machine.

Cook for 5 minutes or until the sandwich maker indicates the toastie is ready. Take the melt out and let it sit for at least 1–2 minutes to cool down slightly. Enjoy!

THE ADVENTURER

This chapter is full of delicious melts inspired by different tastes from around the world. Experience the joy of new flavours from East to West sandwiched between two bits of toasted bread.

4 tbsp butter, at room temperature

16 slices white sourdough bread or 8 ciabatta rolls

400 g (14 oz / 2⅔ cups) grated mozzarella

200 g (7 oz / 1¾ cups) grated mature Cheddar

8 pickled gherkins, sliced (optional)

salt and freshly ground black pepper

PULLED PORK

2 red onions, sliced

2 bay leaves

1 tbsp smoked paprika

good pinch of salt

1 tsp freshly ground black pepper

1.5–2 kg (3¼–4½ lb) skin-on pork shoulder

1 tbsp English mustard

BARBECUE SAUCE

140 g (5 oz) ketchup

2 tbsp red wine vinegar

1 tbsp Worcestershire sauce

3 tbsp soft dark brown sugar

PULLED PORK

PREP TIME:
5 minutes

COOK TIME:
4 hours + 6 minutes

TOASTING METHODS:
F S P

BEST BREAD:
white sourdough or ciabatta roll

Long and slow is a popular way to cook these days; mix that with a beautiful shoulder of pork and some great sourdough bread and you have an awesome toastie, jammed with flavour. Of course, if you have any cooked pork left over from another meal you can make this sandwich really quickly.

Heat the oven to 160°C (320°F / Gas 3).

To cook the pulled pork, scatter the onions and bay leaves in the bottom of a large roasting tin. In a small bowl, mix the paprika with the salt and pepper, then rub the mixture all over the underside of the pork. Turn the pork over and spread the mustard on top, then place it in the roasting tin. Pour 200 ml (7 fl oz) of water into the tin and cover the pork with kitchen foil, wrapping it well over the tin. Bake for 4 hours. The pork can be cooked up to 2 days in advance.

Make the barbecue sauce by slowly bringing all the ingredients to the boil in a small saucepan. Once bubbling, turn the heat down and simmer for 3 minutes until the sauce thickens. Remove from the heat and allow to cool.

Meanwhile, start making the sandwiches. Butter each slice of bread on one side; if you are using ciabatta rolls, split the rolls in half and butter the outside of each slice (not the cut side). Lay 8 slices of the bread, or all the bottom halves of the rolls, butter-side down on a clean work surface.

Divide the pork equally among the laid-out bread, followed by the mozzarella and Cheddar. Add the gherkins if you are using them. Spoon a dollop of the barbecue sauce on top then close the sandwiches with the remaining bread, buttered side facing out.

Heat up a frying pan (skillet) to a medium heat and place the sandwiches in the pan; you will have to cook them in batches so not to overcrowd the pan. Cook for 3 minutes each side until the bread is crisp and golden and the cheese is melting. Remove the toasted sandwiches from the pan and slice them in half. Serve with the rest of the barbecue sauce for dipping. You can also toast the sandwiches in a toasted sandwich maker or panini press.

SEE PHOTO OVERLEAF

2 tbsp olive oil

½ onion, diced

1 garlic clove, grated

250 g (8¾ oz) minced (ground) pork

1 tbsp Worcestershire sauce

25 g (1 oz) Parmesan

freshly ground black pepper

1 tbsp fennel seeds

4 thick slices white bloomer

2 tbsp butter, at room temperature

PICKLED FENNEL

2 tbsp rice vinegar

2 tbsp runny honey

1 small fennel, finely sliced

WALNUT PESTO

45 g (1¾ oz/scant ½ cup) walnut halves

30 g (1 oz) basil leaves

1 tbsp grated Parmesan

60 ml (2 fl oz) olive oil

pinch of sea salt

PORK MEATBALLS PICKLED FENNEL
with WALNUT PESTO

PREP TIME:
20 minutes

COOK TIME:
25 minutes

TOASTING METHOD:

BEST BREAD:
white bloomer

These delicious ingredients are great in a toasted sandwich. It takes a little time to make the meatballs, but time is love and this toastie gives you that with pesto on top!

Make the pickled fennel by mixing the rice vinegar with the honey in a bowl, then add the sliced fennel. Leave to pickle for at least 10 minutes.

Meanwhile, put all the walnut pesto ingredients into a food processor and blend until just combined: the texture should be coarse, not smooth. Set aside.

For the meatballs, heat 1 tablespoon of the oil in a frying pan (skillet) over a medium–low heat, then add the onion and garlic. Gently fry for 5–10 minutes until soft. Remove from the heat and leave to cool.

Put the pork, Worcestershire sauce, Parmesan and onion mixture into a food processor, season with black pepper and blitz until well combined but not completely smooth. Transfer the mixture into a large mixing bowl.

Add the fennel seeds to the pork mixture, combine together using your hands, then form small balls about 2 cm (¾ in) in diameter.

Heat the remaining oil in a large frying pan over a medium heat. Fry the meatballs in batches – it's best not to overcrowd the pan – on all sides for around 10 minutes until golden brown and cooked all the way through.

Toast all 4 slices of bread in a toaster then butter each slice on one side. Lay 1 slice butter-side up, then spread over the walnut pesto followed by the meatballs. Top with the pickled fennel. Repeat this process twice more. You should end up with a stacked meatball sandwich. Cut in half to serve.

SEE PHOTO ON PAGE 55

30 g (1 oz) duck liver pâté
2 thick slices brioche

CARAMELISED ONION
olive oil, for frying
½ small red onion, finely sliced into half moons

BLACK PEPPER BUTTER
1 tbsp butter, at room temperature
½ tsp ground black pepper

DUCK LIVER PÂTÉ BRIOCHE
with CARAMELISED ONION & PEPPER

PREP TIME:
5 minutes

COOK TIME:
15–20 minutes

TOASTING METHOD:

BEST BREAD:
brioche

The richness of duck liver pâté goes extremely well with the caramelised red onion. Feel free to use other types of pâté such as chicken liver or mushroom pâté.

Weigh out the pâté in a small bowl and leave it to one side, covered, while you make the onions and butter so that it's not fridge-cold when you come to use it.

Caramelise the onions by heating some oil in a small saucepan over a medium-low heat. Add the onion and stir to coat it with the oil. Leave to fry gently for 15 minutes, stirring occasionally, or until the onion is soft, browned and slightly sticky. Remove from the heat.

To make the black pepper butter, mix the butter and pepper together in a small bowl until well combined.

Spread the pâté over a slice of the brioche, then spoon the caramelised onion on top. Close the sandwich with the other slice of brioche and spread the pepper butter over the outside of the sandwich.

Heat a frying pan (skillet) to medium-low, add the sandwich and cook for 1 minute. Brioche can easily burn, so keep an eye on it. Flip it over and cook the other side for a further 1 minute. Serve immediately.

250 g (8¾ oz) Portobello mushrooms, cut into 5 mm (¼ in) thick slices

1 onion, sliced (preferably white but you can use any)

½ tbsp thyme leaves

2 tbsp olive oil

4 slices sourdough bread

100 g (3½ oz) taleggio, sliced

salt and freshly ground black pepper

THYME BUTTER

½ tbsp thyme leaves

½ garlic clove, grated

2 tbsp butter, at room temperature

PORTOBELLO MUSHROOM & THYME BUTTER

PREP TIME:
10 minutes

COOK TIME:
25 minutes

TOASTING METHODS:
F S P

BEST BREAD:
sourdough

Roast up these meaty mushrooms for this delicious melt. For a vegan option replace the butter and taleggio with olive oil and a handful of spinach. Season well and it's just as delicious.

Heat the oven to 200°C (400°F / Gas 6).

Scatter the mushrooms and onion into a baking tray, then sprinkle over the thyme leaves and drizzle with the olive oil. Season and roast in the oven for 20 minutes.

Meanwhile, make the thyme butter by mixing all the ingredients together in a small bowl.

Spread the thyme butter on one side of all the slices of bread, then lay them butter-side down. Divide the mushrooms and onions between 2 slices of the bread, top with the taleggio and season. Close the sandwiches with the other slices of bread, butter side facing out.

Heat a frying pan (skillet) over a medium heat and cook the sandwiches for 2–3 minutes on each side. Alternatively, cook them in a toasted sandwich maker or panini press. The bread should be toasted and golden, and the taleggio melted.

50 g (2 oz) new potatoes

1 tsp olive oil

1 tbsp pancetta cubes

2 slices white farmhouse bread

50 g (2 oz/½ cup) grated Comté
(or Gruyère or Swiss cheese)

50 g (2 oz) reblochon, sliced
(or Camembert or brie)

4 cornichons, sliced (optional)

1 tbsp butter, at room temperature

TARTIFLETTE

PREP TIME:
15 minutes

COOK TIME:
15 minutes

TOASTING METHODS:
F S P G

BEST BREAD:
white farmhouse

If you have ever found yourself up a mountain in France, you have probably eaten the moreish tartiflette, made with crispy lardons, soft potatoes and lashings of cheese. Now is your chance to try it sandwiched between crispy golden bread!

Bring a small saucepan of water to the boil and cut any larger new potatoes in half. Put the potatoes into the pan and simmer for around 10 minutes or until they are cooked through. Drain, allow to cool completely, then slice. If you have any cooked new potatoes left over from another meal, you can use these instead.

Heat the olive oil in a frying pan (skillet) and fry the pancetta cubes over a high heat until crispy. Set aside on a piece of paper towel to absorb the excess fat.

Sprinkle the Comté over one slice of the bread, then layer on the sliced potatoes. Scatter over the pancetta, lay on the reblochon and top with cornichons, if using. Put the other slice of bread on top and spread the outside of it with half of the butter. Flip the sandwich over and spread the rest of the butter on the other side.

Heat a frying pan to a medium heat, lay the sandwich in the pan and cook for 3 minutes. Turn the sandwich over and cook for a further 3 minutes or until the bread is golden and crispy and the cheese is melting. You can also cook this sandwich in a toasted sandwich maker or panini press if you prefer. Or, if you prefer, forget the extra slice of bread and cook the melt under a hot grill (broiler). Great served with a crispy green salad.

1 tsp yellow mustard

1 ciabatta or sub roll, halved lengthways

50 g (2 oz/½ cup) grated Gruyère

2 frankfurters, halved lengthways

1½ tbsp sauerkraut

FRANKFURTER, GRUYÈRE & SAUERKRAUT

PREP TIME:
5 minutes

COOK TIME:
5 minutes

TOASTING METHODS:
F S P

BEST BREAD:
ciabatta or sub roll

Three ingredients, made for each other with a little bit of mellow yellow mustard. This will make your mouth zing!

Spread the mustard on one half of the bread and sprinkle half of the cheese over the top.

Add the frankfurters, then spread the sauerkraut over the top and finish with the rest of the cheese. Close the sandwich.

Heat a frying pan (skillet) to medium-hot and put the sandwich into the pan. Let it cook for 3 minutes on one side, then turn the sandwich over and cook for 2 minutes on the other side. The bread should be crispy and the cheese gooey. Alternatively, cook the sandwich in a toasted sandwich maker or a panini press.

2 slices smoked streaky bacon

olive oil, for frying

5 fresh or ready-cooked king prawns (jumbo shrimp)

1 tbsp mayonnaise

2 thick slices white farmhouse bread

handful of rocket (arugula)

1 tbsp butter, at room temperature

1 garlic clove, peeled

KING PRAWN, BACON & GARLIC

PREP TIME:
5 minutes

COOK TIME:
15–20 minutes

TOASTING METHODS:
F S P

BEST BREAD:
white farmhouse

This is a posh toastie that gives a hit of smoky saltiness along with umami sweetness. Served with Seasonal Slaw (see page 24), this is a fantastic meal.

Cook the bacon either in a frying pan (skillet) or under the grill (broiler) until crispy and set aside.

Heat a little oil in a frying pan over a medium–high heat and fry the raw prawns for 3–6 minutes until they are pink and cooked through, or fry the cooked prawns until they are hot.

Spread the mayonnaise on one slice of the bread. Add the crispy bacon, then top with the prawns and rocket. Place the other slice of bread on top, then spread half of the butter on top of the sandwich. Carefully flip it over and spread the rest of the butter on the other side.

Heat a clean frying pan until medium-hot and put the sandwich in the pan. Fry for 2–3 minutes on each side until crisp and golden. Alternatively, cook the sandwich in a toasted sandwich maker or panini press.

Remove the toastie from the pan or machine and lightly rub the garlic clove all over it. Cut in half to serve.

1 tbsp mayonnaise

2 slices multiseed bread

½ avocado, sliced

1½ tsp dukkah

30 g (1 oz) Parmesan, sliced

5 basil leaves

small handful of baby spinach leaves

1 tbsp butter, at room temperature

SPINACH, AVOCADO & DUKKAH

PREP TIME:
5 minutes

COOK TIME:
6 minutes

TOASTING METHODS:
🍞 🥪 🥖

BEST BREAD:
multiseed

A delicious, fresh-tasting melt with an element of green. The dukkah adds that extra crunch.

Spread the mayonnaise on one slice of the bread and top with the avocado. Sprinkle over the dukkah and lay the Parmesan and basil leaves on top. Top with the spinach and close the sandwich with the other slice of bread. Spread both sides of the sandwich with the butter.

Heat a pan over a medium heat and lay the sandwich in the pan. Cook each side for 2–3 minutes or until the outside is crispy and the Parmesan has melted. Alternatively, cook the sandwich in a toasted sandwich maker or panini press. Slice in half and serve.

100 g (3½ oz) Chantenay carrots, tops removed and halved lengthways

¼ tsp crushed chilli (red pepper flakes)

5 sprigs thyme

1 tbsp runny honey

1 tbsp olive oil

2 tbsp butter, at room temperature

zest of ½ lemon

4 slices multigrain or granary bread

100 g (3½ oz) soft goat's cheese

1 tbsp milk

freshly ground black pepper

1 tbsp salted pistachios, chopped

ROASTED CARROT & WHIPPED GOAT'S CHEESE

PREP TIME:
10 minutes

COOK TIME:
25 minutes

TOASTING METHODS:
F S P

BEST BREAD:
multigrain or granary

A delicious sweet veggie toastie with a few nuts and seeds to boot!

Heat the oven to 200°C (400°F / Gas 6).

Scatter the carrots, crushed chilli and thyme into a baking tray, then drizzle over the honey and olive oil. Stir well to coat the carrots, then roast in the oven for 15 minutes.

Meanwhile, mix the butter with half of the lemon zest and spread it on one side of each slice of bread. Lay the bread butter-side down on a clean work surface or plate.

Put the goat's cheese, the remaining lemon zest, the milk and some black pepper into the bowl of a food processor and whip for 1 minute on high speed.

Spread the whipped goat's cheese mixture on 2 slices of the bread. Sprinkle over the pistachios and then lay the carrots on top. Close the sandwich with the other slices of bread, butter sides facing out.

Heat a large frying pan (skillet) to a medium heat and cook the sandwiches for 2–3 minutes on each side or until the bread is golden and crispy. You can also cook the sandwiches in a toasted sandwich maker or panini press if you have one.

3 slices smoked streaky bacon

30 g (1 oz) Gouda, sliced

2 slices white sourdough bread

30 g (1 oz) mature Cheddar, sliced

½ apple, sliced (preferably Granny Smith)

freshly ground black pepper

1 tbsp butter, at room temperature

SMOKED BACON, APPLE & CHEESE

PREP TIME:
10 minutes

COOK TIME:
15 minutes

TOASTING METHODS:
F S P

BEST BREAD:
white sourdough

Salty, smoky, sweet and gooey. Vital components of a great toasted sandwich. Serve with a side of Seasonal Slaw (see page 24).

Cook the bacon either in a frying pan (skillet) or under the grill (broiler) until crispy.

Lay the Gouda on one slice of the bread, then add the bacon, Cheddar and sliced apple. Season with black pepper and top with the other slice of bread. Butter the top of the sandwich, then carefully turn it over and butter the other side.

Heat a griddle pan over a medium–high heat and lay the sandwich in the pan. Fry each side for 3 minutes or until the melt is crispy on the outside and gooey in the middle. Alternatively, toast the sandwich in a toasted sandwich maker or panini press.

100 g (3½ oz/generous ½ cup)
tenderstem broccoli

2 tbsp butter, at room temperature

4 slices multiseed or brown bread

2 tbsp chilli jam or chutney

1 × approx. 200 g (7 oz) burrata

sea salt and freshly ground
black pepper

TENDERSTEM BROCCOLI & BURRATA

PREP TIME:
10 minutes

COOK TIME:
10 minutes

TOASTING METHODS:
F S P

BEST BREAD:
multiseed or brown

Burrata is a ball of mozzarella filled with cream – when melted it's a dream. Paired with crunchy broccoli and a hint of chilli, this sandwich really rocks.

Bring a medium saucepan of water to the boil. Add the broccoli and cook for 3 minutes until just tender. Drain and set aside.

Butter each slice of bread on one side and lay them butter-side down on a clean work surface or plate. Spread the chilli jam or chutney onto the unbuttered side of 2 slices of the bread.

Cut the burrata in half, being careful not to spill the cream in the middle all over the place. Put one half in the middle of each jam-covered slice of bread, cut side up. Top with the broccoli and season. Put the remaining slices of bread on top with the buttered sides facing out.

Heat a large frying pan (skillet) to a medium heat and place the sandwiches in the pan. Cook for 3 minutes, then flip the sandwiches over and cook the other sides for a further 2–3 minutes or until the toast is crispy and the burrata melted. Alternatively, cook the sandwiches in a toasted sandwich maker or a panini press.

CHEESETASTIC

A whole chapter devoted to the best cheesy melts you have ever tasted. From Gorgonzola to manchego, vintage Cheddar to Stilton, plus halloumi, feta and brie. If you are a big fan of cheese, look no further.

2 tbsp butter, at room temperature

4 slices rye sourdough or brown bread

1 garlic clove, peeled

100 g (3½ oz) mature Cheddar, thinly sliced

freshly ground black pepper

chutney, to serve (optional)

gherkin, sliced, to serve (optional)

MATURE CHEDDAR & GARLIC

PREP TIME:
5 minutes

COOK TIME:
10 minutes

TOASTING METHODS:
F S P

BEST BREAD:
sourdough or brown

A good mature Cheddar should make your mouth water uncontrollably. If you are making this in spring, try using wild garlic instead of a clove.

Butter each slice of bread on one side and place butter-side down on a clean work surface or plate. Cut the clove of garlic in half and gently rub the cut side of the garlic over the unbuttered sides of the bread.

Lay the cheese over 2 slices of bread, season with pepper and top with the other slices of bread, butter-sides facing out.

Heat a large heavy-based frying pan over a low-medium heat. Place the sandwiches in the pan, butter-side down, and fry for 3–5 minutes until golden on the outside and the cheese is partially melted on the inside. Flip over and fry for another 3–5 minutes to cook the other side until toasted and golden on both sides and the cheese is fully melted. Alternatively, cook the sandwiches in a toasted sandwich maker or panini press. Serve with chutney and slices of gherkins, if desired.

1 red (bell) pepper

1 cooking chorizo, halved lengthways and sliced

1 tbsp butter, at room temperature

2 slices rye sourdough or brown bread

1 tbsp mayonnaise

small handful of rocket (arugula)

30 g (1 oz) manchego, sliced

MANCHEGO & CHORIZO

PREP TIME:
15 minutes

COOK TIME:
30–40 minutes

TOASTING METHODS:
F S P

BEST BREAD:
rye, sourdough or brown

Manchego is a fantastic sheep's cheese from Spain and is very high in protein. This means it doesn't like high cooking temperatures, but that doesn't stop it from delivering a great flavour in this toastie, especially when teamed up with chorizo.

Heat the oven to 200°C (400°F / Gas 6) and place the pepper onto a small baking tray. Roast the pepper for 20–25 minutes until soft. Remove from the oven and leave to cool, then slice, discarding the core and seeds.

Heat a frying pan (skillet) over a medium-high heat and fry the chorizo for 3 minutes each side or until cooked through. Set aside.

Spread the butter over each slice of bread and turn them over. Spread one slice with the mayonnaise and top with the rocket. Lay the manchego on top, then the pepper and the hot chorizo. Close the sandwich with the other slice of bread, butter-side up, and press down with a spatula.

Heat another frying pan over a medium heat and cook the sandwich for 3–4 minutes on each side until the cheese has melted and the bread is toasted and golden. You can also cook the sandwich in a toasted sandwich maker or a panini press.

2 tbsp butter, at room temperature

1 leek, sliced

1 medium baguette

30 g (1 oz) mature Cheddar, sliced

20 g (¾ oz) Comté, sliced

15 g (½ oz) Gruyère or ogleshield

freshly ground black pepper

TRIPLE CHEESE & LEEK

PREP TIME:
10 minutes

COOK TIME:
20 minutes

TOASTING METHODS:

BEST BREAD:
baguette

Yes, that's right – three cheeses in one sandwich. As for the types of cheese, not everyone has these in their fridge but, if you get time, do try and search these out. Serve with a side of Carrot Caraway Fries (see page 26).

Melt 1 tablespoon of the butter in a frying pan (skillet) over a low heat. Add the leek and cook gently for 15 minutes until soft, stirring occasionally. Meanwhile, slice the baguette lengthways, butter the outside of each half and lay them butter-side down.

Spoon the leeks onto one half of the baguette, evenly layer on all the cheeses and season with pepper. Top with the remaining half of the baguette, butter side facing out.

Heat a heavy-based frying pan over a medium heat. Fry the sandwich in the pan for 3 minutes, then flip it over, press down using a spatula and cook for a further 2–3 minutes. If the cheese isn't melted enough before you flip the sandwich, reduce the heat and cook for a bit longer on both sides. Alternatively, cook the sandwich in a panini press until golden and crisp on the outside and the cheese is melted on the inside. Slice and serve.

1 tbsp butter, at room temperature

1 tsp thyme leaves

2 slices white sourdough bread

3 tbsp soft goat's cheese

1 medium pickled beetroot (beet), sliced

small handful of rocket (arugula)

sea salt and freshly ground black pepper

GOAT'S CHEESE & PICKLED BEETROOT

PREP TIME:
10 minutes

COOK TIME:
6 minutes

TOASTING METHODS:
F S P

BEST BREAD:
white sourdough

Try pickling the beetroot (beet) yourself for the best flavour, otherwise simply use one from a jar. To make a quick pickle, cook the beetroot in a small saucepan of boiling water until tender, then drain, cool and slice. Mix 3 tablespoons of rice vinegar with 1 tablespoon of maple syrup or honey in a small bowl. Add the beetroot and drown it in the vinegar mix for 10 minutes. Boom ... You have a pickle! Goat's cheese loves beetroot and this melted sandwich is a good example.

In a small bowl, mix the butter with the thyme leaves. Spread the thyme butter on one side of both slices of bread and place the bread butter–side down.

Spread the goat's cheese on one slice of the bread, top with the pickled beetroot and add the rocket. Season well with salt and pepper, then close the sandwich with the other slice of bread, butter side face up.

Heat a heavy-based frying pan over a medium heat and cook the sandwich for 3 minutes on each side, gently pressing down on it with a spatula to help it crisp up. You can also cook the sandwich in a toasted sandwich maker or panini press if you prefer. Slice in half and serve.

4 slices bacon

4 slices brown sourdough bread

120 g (4¼ oz) vintage Cheddar, sliced

handful of rocket (arugula)

sea salt and freshly ground black pepper

BLOODY MARY BUTTER

4 tbsp butter, at room temperature

1 tbsp tomato purée (paste)

1 tsp Worcestershire sauce

4 drops of Tabasco sauce

VINTAGE CHEDDAR, BLOODY MARY BUTTER, BACON & ROCKET

PREP TIME:
15 minutes

COOK TIME:
10–15 minutes

TOASTING METHODS:
🅕 🅢 🅟

BEST BREAD:
brown sourdough

This early morning hangover melt is the perfect cure.

Cook the bacon using your preferred method, until nice and crispy. Set aside.

To make the Bloody Mary Butter, mix 2 tablespoons of the butter in a bowl with the tomato purée, Worcestershire sauce and Tabasco. Pop the Bloody Mary butter in the fridge and chill for 10 minutes.

Meanwhile, spread the remaining butter on one side of each slice of bread and lay them butter side down.

Spread the Bloody Mary butter on the unbuttered sides of the bread, then lay the cheese on 2 of the slices. Season, top with the bacon and rocket, and close the sandwiches with the remaining bread so that the Bloody Mary butter is on the inside and the plain buttered sides are facing out.

Heat a large heavy-based frying pan (skillet) on a medium heat and transfer the sandwiches into the pan. Cook for 3 minutes then flip them over and cook for a further 2–3 minutes or until the cheese has melted and the bread is crispy and golden. Alternatively, cook the sandwiches in a toasted sandwich maker or in a panini press if you have one.

1 tbsp butter, at room temperature

2 slices white sourdough bread

1 tsp sriracha

25 g (1 oz/¼ cup) grated mature Cheddar

25 g (1 oz) Stilton or other blue cheese, sliced or crumbled

70 g (2½ oz) kimchi, finely chopped (available online or at Asian supermarkets)

½ spring onion (scallion), finely sliced

SPICED STILTON, CHEDDAR & KIMCHI

PREP TIME:
10 minutes

COOK TIME:
6 minutes

TOASTING METHODS:
F S P

BEST BREAD:
white sourdough

Not for the faint-hearted, but if you are willing to try it you are bound to love it!

Spread the butter onto one side of both slices of bread and place them butter-side down on a plate. Drizzle the sriracha over one slice, then layer on the Cheddar, Stilton, kimchi and spring onion. Top with the second slice of bread, butter side face up.

Heat a griddle pan or heavy-based frying pan (skillet) over a medium heat. Lay the sandwich in the pan and press down with a spatula. Cook for 3 minutes, then flip over and cook for a further 3 minutes or until the outside is golden and the cheese has melted. Alternatively, cook the sandwich in a toasted sandwich maker or a panini press. Slice in half and serve.

2 slices rye bread or rye sourdough bread

2 tbsp cream cheese

a few dill fronds, to serve

freshly ground black pepper

PICKLED CUCUMBER

2 tbsp rice vinegar

1 tsp maple syrup

¼ cucumber, sliced

CREAM CHEESE & PICKLED CUCUMBER

PREP TIME:
12 minutes

COOK TIME:
2 minutes

TOASTING METHOD:

BEST BREAD:
rye or rye sourdough

Pickled cucumber is a fantastic aid to a grilled cheese sandwich. They bring crunch and a burst of sour juice, which sits ever so well with creamy cheese. Try this on for size.

To make the pickled cucumber, mix together the rice vinegar and maple syrup in a small bowl. Submerge the sliced cucumber in the pickling mixture and leave for 10 minutes.

Toast the rye bread in a toaster until it's nice and crunchy.

Working quickly, spread the cream cheese over your slices of toast, add the sliced cucumber and sprinkle with the dill. Crack over some black pepper and serve.

2 tbsp extra-virgin olive oil

1 garlic clove, grated

2 generous handfuls of kale leaves, chopped

4 thick slices white farmhouse bread

120 g (4¼ oz / 1¼ cups) grated Gouda

sea salt and freshly ground black pepper

GOUDA & KALE

PREP TIME:
10 minutes

COOK TIME:
12 minutes

TOASTING METHODS:
F S P

BEST BREAD:
white farmhouse

The king of green, kale deserves a place in a toastie, especially sandwiched with a good cheese like creamy Gouda. Kids can't say no to a cheese sandwich, even if there is a bit of green.

Heat 1 tablespoon of the oil in a frying pan (skillet) over a medium-high heat. Fry the garlic for 30 seconds, then add the kale. Cook for 3–4 minutes or until the kale softens and wilts, stirring occasionally. Season and remove from the heat.

Brush one side of each slice of bread with the remaining olive oil and lay them oil-side down. Distribute the kale over 2 slices of the bread, sprinkle over the gouda and top with the remaining bread, oil-side up.

Heat a heavy-based frying pan over a medium heat, then lay the sandwiches in the pan. Cook for 3 minutes, then flip them over and cook for a further 4 minutes until they are golden and crispy on the outside and the cheese has melted inside. Alternatively, cook the sandwiches in a toasted sandwich maker or panini press until golden and melted.

100 g (3½ oz / 2⅔ cups) diced
pumpkin or squash

olive oil, for roasting

2 tsp lemon thyme, finely chopped,
plus extra to garnish

2 tbsp butter, at room temperature

4 slices multiseed bread

100 g (3½ oz / ⅓ cup) ricotta

large handful of rocket (arugula)

sea salt and freshly ground
black pepper

RICOTTA & PUMPKIN
with LEMON THYME BUTTER

PREP TIME:
10 minutes

COOK TIME:
30–35 minutes

TOASTING METHODS:
🅕 🅢 🅟

BEST BREAD:
multiseed

Flavoured butter is a great way to add an extra burst of taste.
Lemon thyme works really well here, but also try out rosemary
and other hardy herbs; soft herbs like basil will burn.

Preheat the oven to 200°C (400°F / Gas 6). Scatter the pumpkin
or squash into a small baking tray. Drizzle with olive oil and roast
in the oven for 25–30 minutes, stirring halfway through, until
cooked and softened. Set aside.

In a small bowl, mix the lemon thyme with the butter. Spread the
lemon thyme butter onto one side of each slice of bread and lay
them butter-side down on a clean work surface.

Spread 2 slices of the bread with the ricotta and sprinkle with
more lemon thyme. Add the pumpkin and rocket, then season.
Top with the remaining bread, with the buttered sides facing out.

Heat a large heavy-based frying pan (skillet) over a medium heat
and lay the sandwiches in the pan. Press down on them with a
spatula and cook for 3 minutes. Flip them over and cook for a
further 2–3 minutes, pressing down with the spatula again to
help crisp up the bread. They are ready when toasted and golden.
You can also cook the sandwiches in a toasted sandwich maker
or panini press.

60 g (2¼ oz) halloumi
1 tbsp butter, at room temperature
2 slices white sourdough bread
small handful of spinach
1 tbsp chopped mint leaves
1 tbsp pickled jalapeño

SQUEAKY CHEESE
with JALAPEÑO & MINT

PREP TIME:
12 minutes

COOK TIME:
10 minutes

TOASTING METHODS:
F S P

BEST BREAD:
white sourdough

Halloumi is that famous squeaky Greek cheese, which adds a fantastic salty note to any sandwich. You can griddle it first for flavour, as this cheese won't ooze.

Cut the halloumi into 3 slices and dry fry it in a frying pan (skillet) or griddle pan over a medium-high heat for 2 minutes on each side.

Spread the butter on one side of both slices of bread and lay them butter-side down. Lay the halloumi on one of the slices, then add the spinach, mint and jalapeños. Put the other slice of bread on top, with the butter side face up.

Heat a heavy-based frying pan over a medium-high heat, then transfer the sandwich into the pan. Cook for 3 minutes, pressing down with a spatula to help the bread toast, then flip it over and cook for a further 3 minutes until the sandwich is golden and crispy. Alternatively, cook the sandwich in a toasted sandwich maker or a panini press.

1 tbsp pine nuts

2 slices rye sourdough bread

1 tbsp butter, at room temperature

50 g (2 oz) Gorgonzola, sliced

PICKLED PEAR

2 tbsp rice vinegar

1 tsp honey

½ pear, cored and thinly sliced

GORGONZOLA, PINE NUT & PICKLED PEAR

PREP TIME:
10 minutes

COOK TIME:
10 minutes

TOASTING METHODS:
F S P

BEST BREAD:
rye, sourdough

Tangy and delicious, this rich, creamy blue cheese from Italy is fantastic in a melt. A quick pickled pear marries brilliantly here.

Toast the pine nuts in a small dry frying pan (skillet) over a medium heat for about 5 minutes, shaking the pan occasionally so the kernels don't burn, until golden all over. Transfer the pine nuts to a bowl and set aside.

Mix the rice vinegar and honey together in a small bowl. Submerge the sliced pear in the liquid and leave for 2–3 minutes.

Butter both slices of sourdough on one side and lay them butter-side down. Put the Gorgonzola on one of the slices, then lay the pickled pear on top. Carefully sprinkle over the pine nuts, drizzle over some of the vinegar and honey liquid, and top with the other slice of bread, buttered side facing out.

Heat a heavy-based frying pan over a medium heat and transfer the sandwich into the pan. Fry for 3 minutes, pressing down with a spatula to help it cook, then turn the sandwich over and cook for another 2–3 minutes. It's ready to serve when the bread is golden and crispy on the outside and the cheese is melted on the inside. You can also cook the sandwich in a toasted sandwich maker or panini press if you prefer. Eat this as an open-faced sandwich if you like!

3 slices smoked streaky bacon

1 tbsp butter, at room temperature

2 slices white farmhouse bread
or bloomer

1 tbsp raspberry jam (jelly)

60 g (2¼ oz) Brie, sliced

BRIE & BACON

PREP TIME:
8 minutes

COOK TIME:
10 minutes

TOASTING METHODS:
F S P

BEST BREAD:
white farmhouse or
bloomer

This delicious melt can be varied to suit what you fancy. You can use a different jam (jelly), from fig to strawberry, or you could add freshly sliced strawberries or pears instead – it's up to you.

Cook the bacon either in a frying pan (skillet) or under the grill (broiler) until crispy. Set aside.

Butter one side of both slices of bread and lay them butter-side down. Spread the jam over one of the unbuttered sides of bread, then top with the Brie and bacon. Close the sandwich with the other slice of bread, with the buttered side facing out.

Heat a heavy-based frying pan over a medium-high heat and lay the sandwich in the pan. Press down with a spatula and cook for 3 minutes, then flip the sandwich over and cook for a further 2–3 minutes or until golden on the outside and the brie is melted and oozing in the middle. Alternatively, cook the sandwich in a toasted sandwich maker or panini press.

2

1 red (bell) pepper

2 tbsp butter, at room temperature

4 slices multiseed bread

4 tbsp hummus

100 g (3½ oz) feta

freshly ground black pepper

FETA, HUMMUS & RED PEPPER

PREP TIME:
10 minutes

COOK TIME:
25–30 minutes

TOASTING METHODS:
F S P

BEST BREAD:
multiseed

Feta doesn't melt much, but it does heat up and create a special hot saltiness. Combined with hummus and roasted red peppers, this toastie has a well-deserved spot in this book.

Heat the oven to 200°C (400°F/Gas 6). Place the pepper into a small baking tray and roast it in the oven for 20–25 minutes until soft. Remove from the oven, allow to cool and then slice. Discard the core and seeds.

Butter one side of each slice of bread and lay them butter-side down on a clean work surface. Spread the hummus over 2 of the slices, then crumble over the feta. Divide the roasted peppers on top and add the remaining slices of bread with the buttered sides facing out. Grind over some black pepper.

Heat a heavy-based frying pan (skillet) over a medium heat. Put the sandwich into the pan and cook for 3 minutes, pressing down with a spatula, then flip it over and cook for a further 2–3 minutes until golden and crispy. Alternatively, you can cook this sandwich in a toasted sandwich maker or panini press.

HUNGRY

Ravenous cravings are enjoyably quashed
right here. With double carb options and
full-flavoured fillings, this chapter delivers.
If you want to chuck everything at a
grilled sandwich, this is where it happens.

1 large potato

1 tsp yellow mustard seeds

2 curry leaves, crumbled (optional)

½ red onion, finely chopped

½ tsp ground turmeric

1 green chilli, finely chopped

2 cm (¾ in) piece ginger,
finely chopped

4 small chapatis or flour tortillas
(or 2 large chapatis or flour
tortillas, halved)

3 tbsp vegetable oil

2 tbsp mango chutney, plus extra
to serve

1 tsp sea salt

sour cream or yoghurt, to serve
(optional)

BOMBAY MASALA
OR SPICED POTATO

PREP TIME:
10 minutes

COOK TIME:
25–35 minutes

TOASTING METHOD:
🍳

BEST BREAD:
chapati or flour tortilla

Partial to a bit of Indian spice? This sandwich hits the spot with
aromatic curry leaves and flavour-popping mustard seeds. Top it
off with mango chutney and you have the full package.

Bring a saucepan of water to the boil and cook the potato with
its skin on for 20–30 minutes until tender; don't let it get too
soft. Drain, allow to cool slightly, then peel off the skin while
it's still warm. Leave to cool completely, then grate it into a bowl.

Mix the mustard seeds, curry leaves (if using), red onion, turmeric,
chilli and ginger into the grated potato.

Brush one side of each chapati or tortilla with some of the oil.

Put a heavy-based frying pan (skillet) over a medium heat and
lay a flatbread, oil side down, in the pan. Spread half of the
mango chutney over it, then add half of the potato mixture and
season with salt. Top with another flatbread and press down with
a spatula. Cook for 3 minutes, then turn the sandwich over and
cook for a further 2–3 minutes or until crispy on the outside and
the potato is warmed through. Transfer the toastie to a warmed
plate and cover it with kitchen foil to keep hot while you make
the other sandwich. Assemble and cook it the same way using the
remaining ingredients. Slice into pieces and serve with sour cream
or yoghurt and more mango chutney, if desired.

4

4 ciabatta rolls, halved

40 g (1½ oz/⅓ cup) grated Parmesan

150 g (5¼ oz) mozzarella, sliced

8 basil leaves

BEEF RAGÙ

1 tbsp olive oil

1 small onion, chopped

1 medium red (bell) pepper, chopped

250 g (8¾ oz) extra-lean minced (ground) beef

1 garlic clove, grated

1 tbsp tomato purée (paste)

250 ml (8½ fl oz) passata (puréed tomatoes)

1 tbsp brown sugar

1 tsp Worcestershire sauce

pinch of dried Italian herbs

1 tsp red wine vinegar

sea salt and freshly ground black pepper

BEEF RAGÙ & CHEESE

PREP TIME:
10 minutes

COOK TIME:
35 minutes

TOASTING METHOD:
Ⓖ

BEST BREAD:
ciabatta roll

Ever wondered what to do with a leftover bolognese? Well look no further. This meaty melt practically makes itself for you, if you have some left from the night before. If not, simply follow this quick ragù recipe and take yourself to Italian toastie heaven.

To make the beef ragù, heat the oil in a large heavy-based saucepan over a medium–high heat. Add the onion and red pepper and fry for 5 minutes, stirring occasionally.

Add the beef and break it apart with a wooden spoon. Mix in the garlic, then cook the beef for about 6 minutes until browned, only stirring it when the meat starts sticking to the bottom of the pan; browning the beef like this really enhances its flavour.

Stir in the tomato purée, passata, brown sugar, Worcestershire sauce, herbs and red wine vinegar, and season. Bring the sauce to the boil, then reduce the heat to low. Simmer for 15 minutes, stirring occasionally. Remove from the heat and allow to rest.

Heat the grill (broiler) to medium–high and lay the ciabatta rolls, cut-side up, on a baking tray. Toast for 3–4 minutes, then remove from the heat and lay a slice of mozzarella on one half, and a spoonful of the ragù on top. Sprinkle each one with Parmesan and garnish with the basil. Close the sandwiches with the ciabatta tops and put them back under the grill for 3–4 minutes until the cheese has melted and the bread is golden.

250 g (8¾ oz) cauliflower, grated

130 g (4½ oz/1 cup) grated firm mozzarella

100 g (3½ oz/1¼ cup) grated mature Cheddar

60 g (2¼ oz/1⅔ cup) grated Parmesan

2 large eggs

1 spring onion (scallion), finely chopped

1 tsp Dijon mustard

2 tbsp chopped chives

2 tbsp chopped parsley

2 large tomatoes, thickly sliced

1 tbsp sugar

1 tbsp olive oil

sea salt and freshly ground black pepper

CAULIFLOWER WAFFLES
with SLOW-ROASTED TOMATOES & CHEESE

PREP TIME:
10 minutes

COOK TIME:
20 minutes

TOASTING METHOD:
W

This takes the toasted sandwich to another level. Made without any bread, these crispy waffles with oozy cheese are a perfect gluten-free option, but everyone must try them at least once!

Put the grated cauliflower into a saucepan with 2 tablespoons of water, bring it to the boil and cook until the water evaporates. The cauliflower pieces should be tender – if they're still firm, add another tablespoon of water and cook this water off too.

Put 100 g (3½ oz) of the mozzarella into the bowl of a food processor, along with the cooked cauliflower, Cheddar, Parmesan, eggs, spring onion, mustard and herbs. Blend until smooth.

Heat up a waffle iron, then spoon in the batter, making sure not to overload it. Cook for about 8 minutes in an electric iron, or around 8 minutes on each side in a stovetop iron, until the waffles are crisp and golden.

Meanwhile, heat the grill (broiler) to a high heat. Lay the tomatoes on a baking sheet, sprinkle them with the sugar, drizzle over the olive oil and season. Grill for 10 minutes or until soft. Transfer the waffles to a plate and put the tomatoes on top of 2 of them. Sprinkle over the rest of the mozzarella and gently press the other waffles down on top. Serve straight away.

1 medium potato, peeled

1 tbsp olive oil

1 red onion, sliced

2 tbsp butter, at room temperature

1 tsp chopped rosemary

2 thick slices white bread

30 g (1 oz) Fontina, sliced

sea salt and freshly ground
black pepper

CRISPY POTATO & FONTINA

PREP TIME:
5 minutes

COOK TIME:
30 minutes

TOASTING METHOD:

BEST BREAD:
white

This is a special toastie trick with mashed potato. Don't use instant mash; you must use proper mash otherwise you won't get the required crispiness.

Bring a small saucepan of water to the boil. Halve the potato, place them in the hot water and boil for 15–20 minutes or until tender but not falling apart.

While the potato is cooking, heat the olive oil in a frying pan (skillet) over a low heat, then add the onion. Fry for 15 minutes until the onion is soft and lightly coloured, stirring occasionally; you want the onion to sweeten in its natural sugars rather than crisp up. Remove from the heat and set aside.

Drain the potato, then return it to the saucepan. Add 1 tablespoon of the butter and season. Mash the potato until it is smooth.

In a small bowl, mix the remaining butter with the rosemary, then spread it over one side of each slice of bread. Lay a slice of the bread butter-side down, then layer over the Fontina and cooked onion. Press the other slice of bread on top, butter side facing up.

Heat up a heavy-based frying pan over a medium heat and transfer the sandwich into the pan. Fry for 2 minutes, then turn it over and cook for a further 2 minutes. Take the sandwich out of the pan but leave the heat on.

Spread 1 tablespoon of the mashed potato on one side of the toasted sandwich. Place it back into the pan potato-side down. Fry for 2 minutes and, while it's frying, spread another tablespoon of mash on top of the sandwich. Flip the toastie over and fry it for a further 2 minutes until the potato is golden and crispy. You can serve any leftover mash on the side or, if there is a lot left, use it to coat another toasted sandwich the next day!

4

8 slices white bread

4 tbsp butter, at room temperature

CARBONARA

350 g (12¼ oz) spaghetti or linguini

2 garlic cloves, peeled

50 g (2 oz) unsalted butter

100 g (3½ oz) pancetta cubes

3 large eggs

50 g (2 oz/1½ cup) grated pecorino

50 g (2 oz/1½ cup) grated Parmesan

sea salt and freshly ground black pepper

CARBONARA

PREP TIME:
15 minutes + cooling time for the pasta

COOK TIME:
15 minutes

TOASTING METHODS:
F S P

BEST BREAD:
white

This classic pasta dish is delicious, and how many times have you added a bit too much pasta so that you have some left over? Well don't throw it away. Refrigerate it. It firms up brilliantly: perfect to add into a sandwich to then be toasted. If you don't have any leftover carbonara, follow this recipe to make it fresh and turn it into a mouth-watering toastie carb-fest for four.

To make the carbonara, bring a large saucepan of water to the boil. Dissolve 1 teaspoon of salt in the water and add the spaghetti. Simmer for 10 minutes or until al dente.

While the pasta is cooking, crush the garlic with the flat side of a large knife to bruise it. Heat a large high-sided frying pan (skillet) over a medium heat and melt the butter. Fry the pancetta and garlic for 5 minutes, stirring often. When the pancetta is golden and crisp, turn the heat right down, remove the garlic with a slotted spoon and discard.

Use tongs to transfer the cooked pasta into the frying pan with the pancetta and toss them together; don't drain the spaghetti first, just lift it straight out of the water. You want some of the cooking liquid to go into the frying pan too as it will start to make the sauce.

Beat and season the eggs in a bowl, then mix in the cheeses. Take the pan of spaghetti and pancetta off the heat and quickly pour the egg mixture into the pan. Use the tongs to lift and stir the spaghetti around the pan so the sauce thickens and everything gets coated. Taste and add more seasoning if needed.

Transfer the carbonara into a large bowl, allow it to cool slightly, then put it in the fridge for at least 15 minutes until it has cooled and firmed up.

Butter each slice of bread on one side and lay 4 of the slices butter-side down. Spoon the carbonara onto the slices, then close the sandwiches with the other slices, buttered sides facing out.

Heat a large heavy-based frying pan over a medium heat. Lay the sandwiches in the pan (you may need to cook them in batches) and press down with a spatula. Cook for 3–4 minutes each side, or until the toast is golden and the carbonara has warmed through inside. Alternatively, cook the sandwiches in a toasted sandwich maker or a panini press.

SEE PHOTO OVERLEAF

4 thick slices white farmhouse bread

1 tbsp grated Parmesan

freshly ground black pepper

MACARONI CHEESE

80 g (2¾ oz/½ cup) macaroni

2 tbsp butter, at room temperature

1 tbsp plain (all-purpose) flour

180 ml (6 fl oz) whole (full-fat) milk

30 g (1 oz/¼ cup) grated mature Cheddar

pinch of English mustard powder

MACARONI CHEESE

PREP TIME:
15 minutes

COOK TIME:
25 minutes

TOASTING METHODS:
F S P

BEST BREAD:
white farmhouse

If you have some mac 'n' cheese left over, brilliant – you are almost there. If not, whip up this much-loved pasta dish and you'll have yourself a mac 'n' Cheddar melt in no time.

To make the macaroni cheese, bring a medium saucepan of salted water to the boil, add the macaroni and cook according to the packet instructions.

Meanwhile, in a large saucepan, melt 1 tablespoon of the butter over a medium heat, then stir in the flour to make a roux. Slowly whisk in the milk to make a smooth sauce. Cook for 3–5 minutes, stirring constantly, until the sauce thickens. Stir in the Cheddar and mustard powder, then take off the heat.

Drain the macaroni and add it to the sauce, and let it sit for 5 minutes so everything thickens up.

Spread the remaining butter on one side of each slice of bread. Lay 2 slices of the bread butter-side down and spoon on the macaroni cheese; be careful not to overload them. If there is too much macaroni cheese to fit in the sandwiches, serve the extra on the side. Sprinkle over the Parmesan and season with black pepper, then top with the remaining slices of bread, buttered sides facing up.

Heat a heavy-based frying pan (skillets) over a medium heat. Carefully transfer the sandwiches into the pan using a spatula. Cook them for 3 minutes on each side, gently pressing down on the bread with the spatula to aid cooking, but not too much as the macaroni may fall out. Alternatively, cook the sandwiches in a toasted sandwich maker or a panini press. The toasties are ready when the bread is golden and crispy.

SEE PHOTO ON PAGE 117

250 g (8¾ oz) mashed potato

30 g (1 oz/¼ cup) plain (all-purpose) flour

1 egg

1 tbsp mayonnaise

2 heaped tbsp sauerkraut

3 slices pastrami

3–4 cornichons, sliced, plus some pickled onions

60 g (2¼ oz) Swiss cheese

sea salt and freshly ground black pepper

POTATO WAFFLES
with PASTRAMI & SAUERKRAUT

PREP TIME:
15 minutes

COOK TIME:
20 minutes

TOASTING METHODS:
W G

The ulti-melt! A classic pastrami and gherkin sandwiched together between two potato waffles. Open wide: this tastes amazing.

Combine the mashed potato with the flour and egg in a bowl and season. Spoon the batter into a waffle iron and cook for 3–5 minutes until the waffles are golden brown.

Turn the grill (broiler) on high to heat up and put the waffles onto a plate or board. Spread the mayonnaise on one waffle and spoon over the sauerkraut. Lay the pastrami on top, then add the cornichons, pickled onions and Swiss cheese. Season.

Close the sandwich with the other waffle and put it under the grill. Grill for 1 minute on each side or until the cheese has melted and the pastrami has warmed through.

4

8 slices bacon

375 g (13¼ oz) mashed potato

250 ml (8½ fl oz) buttermilk

6 medium eggs

60 g (2¼ oz/¼ cup) butter, melted

250 g (8¾ oz/2 cups) plain (all-purpose) flour

1 tsp bicarbonate of soda

½ tsp baking powder (baking soda)

115 g (4 oz/1¼ cup) grated Parmesan

oil for frying

1 avocado, lightly mashed

sea salt and freshly ground black pepper

EGG, BACON & GUACAMOLE WAFFLE

PREP TIME:
15 minutes

COOK TIME:
20–30 minutes

TOASTING METHOD:
Ⓦ

This is a go-to breakfast fit for a king! Bacon, egg and avocado all in one crispy potato waffle. Fills you up and makes you smile.

Cook the bacon either in a frying pan (skillet) or under the grill (broiler) until crispy, then set aside. Heat up the waffle iron.

In a large bowl, whisk together the mashed potato, buttermilk, 2 eggs and the butter until smooth. Add the flour, bicarbonate of soda and baking powder and stir until just combined. Fold in the cheese.

Spoon half of the mixture into the waffle iron – don't overfill – and spread the batter using the back of the spoon. Cook for 5–8 minutes, flipping the iron over halfway through if you're using a stove top iron, or until the waffles are golden and crisp.

Transfer the cooked waffles onto a warmed plate, cover with kitchen foil to keep warm and pour the remaining batter into the iron to cook the rest. Add these to the plate and cover while you heat some oil in a large frying pan over a medium-high heat and fry the remaining eggs to your liking.

Lay the waffles on a board and divide the bacon, avocado and eggs between half of them. Season and top with the other waffles and dive in!

1½ tbsp butter, at room temperature

1 tbsp olive oil

120 g (4¼ oz) boiled potatoes, cut into bite-sized pieces

sea salt and freshly ground black pepper

2 slices smoked streaky bacon, chopped

3 spring onions (scallions), sliced

3 eggs, lightly beaten

1 chilli, sliced (optional)

4 thick slices white bloomer

ketchup or brown sauce, to serve (optional)

BREAKFAST HASH

PREP TIME:
20 minutes

COOK TIME:
20 minutes

BEST BREAD:
white bloomer

TOASTING METHOD:

A hearty breakfast sandwich made with soft white bread, scrambled egg and crispy fried potatoes. Yum.

Heat a large frying pan (skillet) over a medium heat. Melt ½ tablespoon of butter in the pan with the olive oil and fry the potatoes for about 5 minutes, stirring occasionally, until evenly golden all over. Season.

Add the bacon and spring onions, and fry for 1–2 minutes until the bacon is cooked. Turn the heat down and add the eggs. Cook them slowly, stirring occasionally to scramble and make the hash. Remove from the heat, add the chilli (if using) and season well.

Toast the bread, then spread the remaining butter on each slice. Divide the hash between 2 slices of the toast and close the sandwiches with the remaining slices. Serve with ketchup or brown sauce if you wish.

SWEETNESS

Sweet, toasted bread can be just as good
as savoury, claiming a personality all of its
own. Experiment with different flavoured
breads, especially ones embellished with
fruits and nuts. Don't forget the softness
of brioche, which just needs a light bit
of toasting, and makes a perfect vessel
for a pudding. Be warned: softened fruit
in toasties comes out steaming hot! Err
on the side of caution: let them rest for
a minute or two before devouring.

3 peaches, halved and pitted

1½ tbsp maple syrup or clear honey

2 sprigs fresh thyme

125 g (4½ oz/generous ½ cup) mascarpone

½ tbsp icing (confectioners') sugar

½ tsp vanilla extract

2 tbsp butter, at room temperature

1 tsp ground cinnamon

4 slices brioche

CINNAMON-CRUSTED PEACH & MASCARPONE

PREP TIME:
10 minutes

COOK TIME:
25 minutes

TOASTING METHOD:

BEST BREAD:
brioche

Juicy and creamy with a sweet crunch of brioche. A delicious, quick summer dessert.

Heat the oven to 180°C (350°F/Gas 4) and line a baking tray with baking parchment.

Put the peaches on the tray, drizzle them with the maple syrup or honey and top each with a sprig of thyme. Roast for 20 minutes or until the peaches are soft and cooked through, then set aside.

Meanwhile, in a bowl combine the mascarpone with the icing (confectioners') sugar and vanilla, and mix well. In another small bowl, mix together the butter with the cinnamon.

Heat the grill (broiler) to a medium heat. Lay the brioche slices on a baking tray and grill them for 1–3 minutes until lightly golden. Keep an eye on them as brioche cooks quickly. Remove the tray, turn the brioche over and spread the untoasted sides with the cinnamon butter. Return the tray to the grill and toast for another 1–3 minutes until the butter has melted and the brioche slices are golden.

Remove from the grill, turn the slices over and spread the mascarpone mixture on the other side. Lay the roasted peach halves on top and serve.

zest of ⅓ lime

2 tbsp butter, at room temperature

4 slices white bloomer

225 g (8 oz/1 cup) ricotta

115 g (4 oz/⅓ cup) orange marmalade

1 tbsp chopped hazelnuts, toasted, plus extra to serve (optional)

RICOTTA & ORANGE MARMALADE

PREP TIME:
10 minutes

COOK TIME:
6 minutes

TOASTING METHODS:
F S P

BEST BREAD:
white bloomer

Italian ricotta is a great mild cheese and works well in this melt with the bitterness of the marmalade. Don't leave out the lime butter – it gives the toastie that extra punch.

Mix the lime zest with the butter in a small bowl.

Spread the lime butter over one side of each slice of bread, then lay 2 of the slices butter-side down. Spread them with the ricotta, then spoon on the marmalade. Top with the hazelnuts (if using) and the remaining slices of bread, butter-side up. Gently press down on the sandwiches to secure the filling.

Heat a griddle pan to a medium heat and lay the sandwiches in the pan. Griddle for about 3 minutes, then turn the sandwiches over and cook for around 3 minutes more until the filling is warm and the toast is golden. You can also cook the sandwiches in a toasted sandwich maker or a panini press.

Cut in two and serve. Garnish with toasted hazelnuts, if desired

½ tbsp lemon thyme leaves

1 tbsp butter, at room temperature

pinch of sea salt

2 slices multiseed bread

50 g (2 oz/¼ cup) soft goat's cheese

50 g (2 oz/⅓ cup) blueberries

1 tbsp clear honey

BLUEBERRY & GOAT'S CHEESE
with LEMON THYME BUTTER

PREP TIME:
10 minutes

COOK TIME:
5 minutes

TOASTING METHODS:
F S P

BEST BREAD:
multiseed

If you love a bit of goat's cheese, then give this toastie a try! Slightly sour with bursts of blackberry and a sweet drizzle of honey, all toasted between lemon thyme butter.

Mix the lemon thyme in a small bowl with the butter and a pinch of salt, and set aside.

Spread the lemon thyme butter on one side of both slices of bread, then lay one slice butter-side down. Cover it with the goat's cheese, scatter over the blueberries and drizzle with honey. Top with the other slice of bread, butter-side up.

Heat a frying pan over a medium heat, then lay the sandwich in the pan. Fry for 3 minutes, then flip it over and cook the other side for 2–3 minutes or until golden brown. Alternatively, cook the sandwich in a toasted sandwich maker or a panini press. Transfer the sandwich to a plate, slice in half and serve.

4

1 tbsp clear honey, plus extra
to serve

small pinch of salt

60 g (2¼ oz / ½ cup) walnuts,
finely chopped

125 g (4½ oz / ½ cup) cream cheese

4 tbsp butter, at room temperature

8 slices raisin bread (preferably
from a dense loaf)

3 figs, quartered,

2 tbsp light brown sugar (for
closed sandwhich method only)

FIG, WHIPPED CHEESE
& HONEYED WALNUTS

PREP TIME:
15 minutes

COOK TIME:
10–15 minutes

TOASTING METHODS:
T G

BEST BREAD:
raisin

Using flavoured raisin bread sets off this sweet, nutty, cheesy
toastie beautifully. If you fancy making this fruity melt even
more flavoursome, try adding a bit of blue cheese.

Preheat the oven to 180°C (350°F / Gas 4) and line a baking tray
with baking parchment.

Combine the honey and salt in a small bowl, add the walnuts
and toss to coat them in the salted honey. Spread the walnuts
in a single layer on the baking tray. Bake for 5–10 minutes until
toasted, stirring halfway through to ensure they toast evenly.
Remove from the oven and allow to cool.

Whip the cream cheese in a small bowl until light and fluffy.

Toast the slices of bread on a grill (broiler) or in a toaster.

To serve, spread each slice with the whipped cheese, lay the figs
on top, then sprinkle over the toasted walnuts. Drizzle over some
extra honey, then eat!

Alternatively, you can also serve this as a traditional closed
sandwich – just remeber to butter the outside of the bread. I like
to sprinkle over some brown sugar before toasting the bread for a
delicious caramelised flavour.

30 g (1 oz/¼ cup) pecans, chopped

100 g (3½ oz/½ cup) caster (superfine) sugar

1 tsp ground cinnamon

1 tbsp salted butter, at room temperature

2 slices soft white bread

250 ml (8½ fl oz) custard, to serve (optional)

APPLE FILLING

1 Bramley apple, peeled, cored and diced

2 tbsp maple syrup

2 tbsp butter

1–2 tsp lemon juice

APPLE & CINNAMON
with TOASTED PECANS

PREP TIME:
15 minutes

COOK TIME:
20–25 minutes

TOASTING METHODS:
🄵 🅂 🄿

BEST BREAD:
soft white

This spiced, sugary apple toastie is just heavenly when dipped in warm custard.

Make the apple filling by combining all the ingredients in a medium saucepan. Cook over a low heat for 15–20 minutes, stirring occasionally, or until the apples are soft. If there is still a lot of liquid, continue to cook over a low heat until thickened. Turn off the heat and set aside.

While the apples are cooking, toast the pecans in a dry frying pan (skillet) over a medium heat for 3–4 minutes, shaking the pan frequently to ensure they toast evenly. Remove from the heat.

Combine the sugar and cinnamon together in a small bowl. Put 1 tablespoon of the cinnamon sugar into a separate small bowl, add the butter and mix together.

Spread the cinnamon butter over one side of each slice of bread, making sure it reaches right to the corners. Turn one slice over and add the cooked apple. Scatter over the pecans and top with the other slice of bread, butter-side up.

Warm a frying pan over a medium heat and place the sandwich in the pan. Cook for 3 minutes, pressing down on the sandwich with a spatula to help crisp up the bread, or until golden. Flip it over and cook for a further 2 minutes or until both sides are golden and crispy. You can also cook the sandwich in a toasted sandwich maker or panini press if you prefer.

Transfer the toastie to a plate, sprinkle it with the rest of the cinnamon sugar and let it cool for a few minutes: the apple filling will be very hot and can burn your mouth if you bite into it right away! If you are using custard, warm it in a pan or microwave while the toastie cools. Serve the toastie with the custard in a small bowl ready for dipping.

SEE PHOTO OVERLEAF

PUMPKIN WAFFLES

85 g (3 oz / ½ cup) pumpkin, peeled and diced

175 g (6¼ oz / 1¼ cups) spelt flour

40 g (1½ oz / ⅓ cup) cornflour (cornstarch)

140 g (5 oz / 1¼ cups) rolled (porridge) oats

2 tbsp brown sugar

1 tbsp baking powder

1 tsp ground cinnamon

¼ tsp salt

2 eggs

225 ml (7¾ fl oz) whole (full-fat) milk

100 g (3½ oz) Greek yoghurt

3 tbsp coconut oil

1 tsp vanilla extract

CHOCOLATE SAUCE

150 g (5¼ oz) 70% cocoa chocolate, broken into pieces

55 ml (1¾ fl oz) double (heavy) cream

2 tbsp butter

3 tbsp golden syrup

TO SERVE

300 g (10½ oz) salted dulce de leche

vanilla ice cream

SALTED DULCE DE LECHE PUMPKIN WAFFLES

PREP TIME:
25 minutes

COOK TIME:
25–30 minutes

TOASTING METHOD:
Ⓦ

These mini waffles create a delicious toasted sandwich, perfect with a scoop of vanilla ice cream. If you're not into waffles, this is also great made with lightly toasted banana bread.

Steam the pumpkin for the waffles in the microwave or using a stovetop steamer for 10–15 minutes until soft. Transfer to a food processor and blend until smooth. Set aside.

Mix together the flour, cornflour, oats, sugar, baking powder, cinnamon and salt in a large bowl. Whisk in the eggs, milk, yoghurt, oil, vanilla extract and pumpkin purée until well combined. Leave to rest for 15 minutes, heat the waffle iron, and turn on the oven at its lowest temperature.

To make the mini waffles, quickly spoon 2 tablespoons of batter into the waffle iron at regular intervals, leaving space between each one. Cook according to the manufacturer's instructions until golden. Remove the waffles with tongs and put them in an ovenproof dish in the oven to keep warm. Repeat the process until you have used up all the batter; you should end up with about 24 mini waffles. If you don't want to use them all at once, they can be stored for up to 3 months in the freezer.

Make the chocolate sauce by putting the chocolate and cream into a small saucepan. Heat gently, stirring all the time, until the chocolate has melted into the cream. Add the butter and golden syrup, take off the heat and stir through.

To serve, liberally coat half of the waffles with the dulce de leche, add a small scoop of ice cream on top then, working quickly, drizzle the warm chocolate sauce over the top. Close the sandwiches and serve immediately.

SEE PHOTO ON PAGE 139

1 brioche bun

1 tbsp cashew butter

40 g (1½ oz) dark (bittersweet) chocolate

40 g (1½ oz / ⅓ cup) raspberries

1 tsp cocoa powder, to serve (optional)

vanilla ice cream, to serve (optional)

CHOCOLATE, CASHEW BUTTER & RASPBERRIES

PREP TIME:
5 minutes

COOK TIME:
5 minutes

TOASTING METHOD:
G

BEST BREAD:
rye or brioche bun

Fried chocolate bread is pretty special; add some salty cashews and tart raspberries and you've got yourself an amazing sweet melt. Serve with a scoop of vanilla ice cream for an epic dessert.

Slice the brioche bun in half and toast both slices under a grill (broiler) until golden brown and crisp. Spread the cashew butter on the base of the brioche bun, then place the chocolate and raspberries on top. The chocolate should begin to melt from the warmth of the bun.

Place the top half of the brioche bun on top of the chocolaty melt and transfer it to a plate. Serve with a scoop of vanilla ice cream, if desired.

4 apricots, halved and pitted

40 g (1½ oz/¼ cup) unsalted butter, at room temperature

pinch of ground cardamom

2 tbsp butter, at room temperature

4 slices white bloomer

100 g (3½ oz) marzipan, thinly sliced

1 tsp icing (confectioners') sugar to serve

60 ml (2 fl oz) crème fraîche, to serve (optional)

pinch of dried lavender, to serve (optional)

APRICOT FRANGIPANE

PREP TIME:
15 minutes

COOK TIME:
20–25 minutes

TOASTING METHOD:

BEST BREAD:
white bloomer

Baked apricots with almonds are the best of friends. Eat them with marzipan for an absolute delight. Please note, the apricots will be as hot as lava when the toasties are ready, so let them cool for at least a couple of minutes before you dive in.

Heat the oven to 240°C (475°F/Gas 9) and place the apricots, cut side up, in a roasting tray.

Mix the butter with the cardamom in a bowl. Divide the cardamom butter among the apricots, spooning it into the hollows where the stones were. Bake for 10–15 minutes until the apricots are slightly browned, then set them aside to cool.

Meanwhile, butter the bread on one side, then turn the two slices over. Lay the marzipan over the unbuttered sides, top with the apricots and cover with the other slices of bread, butter-side up.

Heat a large frying pan (skillet) or griddle pan over a medium heat, and place the sandwiches in the pan. Press down on them with a spatula to encourage the bread to crisp up and fry for 3 minutes. Turn the sandwiches over and cook for a further 2 minutes or until the bread is golden and the marzipan has warmed through. Transfer the toasties to plates, dust with the icing sugar and serve with crème fraîche sprinkled with dried lavender, if you like.

2 tbsp butter, at room temperature

4 slices white bloomer

70 g (2½ oz/¼ cup) Nutella®

9–14 marshmallows

MALT DRINK

400 ml (13½ fl oz) whole (full-fat) milk

6 heaped tsp Horlicks or Ovaltine

MALTY NUTELLA & MARSHMALLOW

PREP TIME:
5 minutes

COOK TIME:
10 minutes

TOASTING METHODS:

🍞 🥪 🥙

BEST BREAD:
white bloomer

Sweet melts are great for dunking into hot drinks. Try this chocolatey, gooey melt dipped into a large mug of homemade malted milk drink.

Butter the bread on one side right up to the edges, then turn the slices over. Spread the Nutella on all 4 slices of bread, then divide the marshmallows between 2 of them. Cover with the other slices of bread, butter-side up.

Heat a large frying pan (skillet) over a medium heat and place the sandwiches in the pan. Cook for 3 minutes, pressing down on the sandwiches with a spatula to help crisp up the bread. Flip them over and cook for a further 2–3 minutes until golden and crispy on the outside and the marshmallows have melted inside. Alternatively, cook the sandwiches in a toasted sandwich maker or panini press.

Make the malt drink by heating the milk in a saucepan, then mix the powder into the hot milk. Pour into mugs and dip your toastie at your leisure.

1 tbsp butter, at room temperature

2 slices multiseed or brown bread

1 tbsp crunchy peanut butter

1 banana, sliced

PEANUT BUTTER & BANANA

PREP TIME:
5 minutes

COOK TIME:
6 minutes

TOASTING METHODS:
F S P

BEST BREAD:
multiseed or brown

A classic student fix – cheap, tasty and let's not forget: quick!

Butter one side of each slice of bread and lay the bread on a plate butter-side down.

Spread the peanut butter on one slice of the bread, then lay the banana slices on top. Place the other slice of bread on top with the butter-side facing out.

Heat a frying pan (skillet) to medium-hot and transfer the sandwich into the pan. Fry for 3 minutes until that side is golden and toasted, then flip over and fry the other side for another 3 minutes or until the banana has warmed through. You can also cook the sandwich in a toasted sandwich maker or panini press if you prefer. Slice in half and serve.

2 handfuls strawberries

½ tbsp granulated (raw) sugar

2 tbsp butter, at room temperature

1 tsp ground black pepper

4 slices white bloomer

100 g (3½ oz/⅓ cup) cream cheese

MACERATED STRAWBERRIES, CREAM CHEESE & BLACK PEPPER

PREP TIME:
20 minutes

COOK TIME:
6 minutes

TOASTING METHODS:
F S P

BEST BREAD:
white bloomer

Summer sunshine? Make yourself this melt, and enjoy the flavours while you soak up the sun outdoors.

Slice the strawberries in half, or if they are really large, into quarters. Pop them in a bowl and sprinkle with the sugar. Leave for 15 minutes to allow the strawberries to macerate.

Mix the butter with the black pepper in a small bowl and spread over one side of each slice of bread. Turn the two slices over and cover the unbuttered sides with the cream cheese. Top with the macerated strawberries and drizzle any juice at the bottom of the bowl over them.

Warm a large frying pan (skillet) over a medium heat and place the sandwiches into the pan. Cook for 3 minutes and use a spatula to press down on the sandwiches to encourage a golden crust. Flip them over and cook for a further 2–3 minutes until both sides are crisp and golden. You can also cook them in a toasted sandwich maker or a panini press if you have one. Slice in half and serve.

ABOUT THE AUTHOR

Fern Green is a food writer, stylist, and chef living in the UK and Italy. She regularly writes and styles for magazines and works with various high-profile brands on food styling for editorial, advertising and video content. She has written a series of cook books including *Breakfast: Morning, Noon and Night* and *The Mocktail Manual*. During the summer months she cooks for her guests from her Italian kitchen garden at Fireflies and Figs in Central Italy. www.firefliesandfigs.co.uk

THANKS

A big massive thank you to Kate and the team who are always an absolute dream to work with. I would also like to thank my friend Sarah Smith for letting me use her kitchen to test all the recipes.

INDEX

Melts by Fern Green

First published in 2017 by Hardie Grant Books

Hardie Grant Books (UK)
52–54 Southwark Street
London SE1 1UN
hardiegrant.co.uk

Hardie Grant Books (Australia)
Ground Floor, Building 1
658 Church Street
Melbourne, VIC 3121
hardiegrant.com.au

British Library Cataloguing-in-Publication Data. A catalogue
record for this book is available from the British Library.

ISBN: 978-1-78488-089-7

Publisher: Kate Pollard
Senior Editor: Kajal Mistry
Editorial Assistant: Hannah Roberts
Photographer © Jacqui Melville
Art Direction: Nicky Barneby
Food Stylist and Home Economist: Kathy Kordalis
Prop Styling: Ginger Whisk
Author Picture on page 153 © Danielle Wood
Copy editor: Susan Pegg
Proofreader: Kay Halsey
Indexer: Cathy Heath
Colour Reproduction by p2d

Printed and bound in China by 1010

10 9 8 7 6 5 4 3 2 1